12

Who Are You, O Immaculata?

by
Father Karl Stehlin, F. S. S. P. X.

Translated from the German
by Michael J. Miller

Loreto Publications
Fitzwilliam, NH 2007

ALL RIGHTS RESERVED
Published by
Loreto Publications
P. O. Box 603
Fitzwilliam, NH 03447
www.loretopubs.org

ISBN 1-930278-63-2
Printed and bound in the USA

Table of Contents

Part One: The Fundamental Law of Action and Reaction

Part Two: God's Work in the World Through the Immaculata

Part Three:
Creation's Return to God Through the Immaculata

Part Four: The Immaculata in the Mystery of the Most Holy Trinity

Foreword

Who Are You, O Immaculata? by Fr. Karl Stehlin is a valuable book for all Mary's children who want to spend their lives and themselves in her service as her slaves. In every respect this little treatise is composed along the lines of the Marian devotion and mysticism of Saint Louis Marie de Montfort and Saint Maximilian Kolbe, whose writings are quoted extensively. Besides these, it draws on Mary's message at Fatima and thus makes an important connection to the crisis that is convulsing the Church and society today.

In this book moreover, the burning issue of devotion to our Lady is embedded in a Catholic, that is, a comprehensive view of the great plan of creation and God's plan for governing the world: God brings creation into being out of nothing (*actio*); his masterpiece therein, after the humanity of our Lord and Savior, the Immaculata, the daughter of the Father, the mother of the God-man, the bride and sanctuary of the Holy Ghost. She is the prototype of creation, God's original idea of creation in the first place.

Therefore how could she not have a central purpose in the return of creation to God (*reactio*)? In the Holy Sacrifice of the Mass as a sacramental renewal of the sacrifice on the cross, in the seven sacraments of the Church, in doctrine and everywhere in the proclamation of the Faith she has a position that far surpasses all the saints. As Mediatrix of All Graces, Mother of Good Counsel, and Help of Christians she guides the soul that seeks and loves God toward its eternal goal, stands by her people in battle, helps the Church (of which she is the archetype) in her trials today, in her conflict with the forces of darkness, which is in fact assuming apocalyptic proportions.

And so this little book is an appropriate means of enlightening our minds with a better appreciation of the Immaculata, inflaming our hearts with love for her and nourishing our souls with a genuine spirituality.

Blessed the soul whom the Immaculata allows to see her greatness and glory and calls to serve her unconditionally! Blessed the man whom the Immaculata employs as an instrument in carrying out God's plans, in order to perfect her divine Son's work of salvation! Blessed are they who not only are called the children of the Immaculata but are such in spirit and in truth!

Menzingen, in the Month of Mary, May 2006,
Fr. Franz Schmidberger

Introduction

"O Immaculata, Queen of heaven and earth, I know that I am unworthy to draw near to you, to fall down at your feet, with my head bowed to the ground. But because I love you very much, I dare to ask you that you would be so kind as to tell me who you are! For I would like to get to know you better and better, boundlessly, and to love you more and more ardently, without any limits whatsoever. And I long to tell other souls, too, who you are, so that more and more souls might come to know you ever more perfectly and to love you ever more ardently. Indeed, I yearn for you to become the Queen of all the hearts that are beating on earth and ever will beat—and for this to happen as quickly as possible."[1]

"The angels often ask one another: *Quae est ista?* Who can she possibly be? [cf. *Cant.* 3:6; 8:5]. For the Most-High kept her concealed from them. Or if he did reveal anything to them, it was nothing compared to what he withheld."[2]

Again and again we hear from the mouths of the saints the astonished cry: "Who are you, O Immaculata?" Mortal man is speechless before the countless miracles and mysteries that have their origin in her. She stands there alone in her perfection and power as God's masterpiece. The Church praises her

---

1. St. Maximilian Kolbe, fragment of his unfinished book on the Immaculata, August 1940, in: *Błogosławiony Maksymilian Kolbe, Wybór Pism* ["Blessed Maximilian Kolbe: Selected Writings", henceforth: BMK] (Warsaw, 1973), p. .590.
2. St. Louis Marie de Montfort, *True Devotion to the Blessed Virgin* (Bay Shore, NY: Montfort Publications, 1980), par. 3, p. 1.

prerogatives and wants us to honor her more than all the angels and saints (*hyperdulia*). Her role in Christ's work of redemption is unique: she takes part in it as the new Eve and co-Redemptrix; she applies the fruits of redemption to all her children as Mediatrix of All Graces. Thus she is given to us by God as the power through which man is first of all converted, and then as the way by which he comes to Christ. She is the mold of God into which we are poured as "material", so that God may be formed in us by her. We owe to her all the graces that we have received personally. She is also the great sign in the heavens, which leads the Christian army in the combat against Satan. She is victorious in all God's battles. Particularly during the latter times, though, she is there as the last means of salvation that God gives the world. She reveals herself, immediately through her apparitions, indirectly through instruments specially chosen by her to prove her unimaginable power at the moment of the most dreadful attacks of the enemy of souls. Her heart becomes the final refuge of the persecuted and oppressed children of God, who try to stand their ground faithfully beneath the cross of Christ.

Her children, her knights, enlist under her banner; they are her "possession and property" and make up the little army that endures the supreme test and at last is victorious over the superior force arrayed against it, for "in the end my Immaculate Heart will triumph!"

From this perspective it is staggering to contemplate how great, indeed, how limitless a power God willed to give to a mere creature. And the question arises ever more clearly: *Quae est ista?* "Who are you, that you, of all people, will win the victory at the end of the ages? Who are you, that you bear us as our mother, nourish, raise, and guide us and finally promise us victory? You can communicate your immaculate nature to us sinners, but does